As a Man Thinks In His Heart, So Is He

B.C. Harding

To Pat
At Clar Ellagh
On 10ᵉ September 2004
With best wishes
From Ben Harding

New Wine Press

New Wine Press
PO Box 17
Chichester
West Sussex
PO20 6YB
England

ISBN: 1 874367 66 3

Typeset by CRB Associates, Reepham, Norfolk
Printed in England by Clays Ltd, St Ives plc.

Contents

Reasons for writing the book

One Saturday evening I read the words of Proverbs 1:33,

> *'But whoever listens to me will live in safety*
> *and be at ease, without fear of harm.'*

These words offer great comfort but I felt that they were not bringing much comfort to me. Why was this? Did I lack faith? Was my relationship with God skin-deep? Whatever the reason I was unsure of myself.

Then I looked at the words in Hebrews 4:12:

> *'The word of God is living and active. Sharper than any double-edged sword, it penetrates even to dividing soul and spirit, joints and marrow; it judges the thoughts and attitudes of the heart.'*

Why is the Bible sharper than any double-edged sword? The sword can only kill the body but the word of God can penetrate the soul (the mind, the will and the emotions). With the power of the Holy Spirit it can change the way a man thinks. A man's thoughts and attitudes of the heart can be judged when put alongside the Scriptures.

Then I returned to Proverbs 1:33. I realised that the key

for me was to listen to God, to be still, to let Him speak and to allow the words of the Bible to penetrate deep within me.

Living in safety means to be secure. Love and discipline are essential. How much love is there inside me and how much love am I able to give and to receive? How obedient and self-disciplined a person am I? How do my thoughts and the attitudes of my heart compare when put alongside the Scriptures?

If you ask these questions for yourself, I wonder what answers you would come up with! The book will ask many questions of you and may provide some answers.

Acknowledgements

There are many people I would like to thank, especially:

- the children and leaders of St Pancras Explorers, Chichester for their support and encouragement.
- Miss Sally Hockley for typing this manuscript.
- The Reverend Stephen Abbott for his appraisal of the drafts and his constructive comments.

B.C. Harding
June 1997

Introduction

'As a man thinks in his heart, so is he.' (Proverbs 23:7)

A person's life is not primarily made up of the circumstances which surround him. The kind of thoughts which he has determines the kind of world in which he lives. Marcus Aurelius, reputedly the wisest of all the Roman Emperors, wrote:

'Your life is what your thoughts make of it.'

Is it not true that your thoughts affect everything, your attitudes, your goals, your values, your priorities, your choices and your relationships?

The Bible is God's handbook to direct your thinking, to guide you through this life and to point the way to heaven. The aim of the following chapters is to set out some biblical principles and to assist your understanding of God's way for you.

Chapter 1

A New Beginning

'I tell you the truth, unless you change and become like little children, you will never enter the kingdom of heaven.' (Matthew 18:3)

The challenge of these words of Jesus is to change and to become like little children. What does that change mean and why is it so hard for some people to enter the kingdom of heaven? This chapter explores some answers to these questions.

Many people push aside the thought of Christianity because they see it as irrelevant to their lives. So much is happening in the world that there is no time for God. Never has there been such a wide choice of goods to buy, places to visit and varieties of leisure and entertainment to enjoy. Higher standards of living are the goals today, even though this may mean facing the increasing pressures of the rat race. Greater advances in technology, science and medicine have not always succeeded in making the world a happier place; there is still widespread dissatisfaction, disagreement, disease, starvation and despair. Confrontation and exploitation abound; personal communication is poor and relationships break down easily.

Do you sometimes stand back and look at what is happening? Do you question the meaning of life? What answers do you come up with?

God created human beings in His own image, to be like Him. He created us with a mind, free-will and a conscience. He created us to look after the world He had made and gave us power and dominion over it. God also wanted us to listen to Him and obey Him so that everything He had planned would go smoothly. Sadly, we have spoilt the world. We have destroyed much of the natural environment for our own ends and continue to do so. However, dominion brings responsibility and we must give account to God.

Because we have chosen to disobey God, that image in His likeness has been defaced but not destroyed. Because God is holy and we are sinful, we are separated from God – a gulf exists. Despite our efforts to bridge the gulf by good works, religion, philosophy and morality, we have failed. Sin is when we fall short of God's perfect standards and displease Him in our thoughts, in our words and in our deeds, in what we ought to have done and in what we ought not to have done. No one can stand before God in his own righteousness.

'For all have sinned and fall short of the glory of God.'
(Romans 3:23)

We are therefore all condemned.

'For the wages of sin is death, but the gift of God is eternal life in Jesus Christ our Lord.' (Romans 6:23)

Human nature is still the same as it was when Adam and Eve disobeyed God in the Garden of Eden, i.e. a tendency to do evil and to look after self first. Jesus Christ was different. He always put others before Himself. When He spoke publicly, people gathered round to listen to Him and were amazed at His teaching. Early in His ministry, Jesus went to Nazareth where He had been brought up and entered a synagogue on the Sabbath. He read from the scroll of the prophet Isaiah:

> ' "*The Spirit of the Lord is upon me,*
> *because he has anointed me*
> *to preach good news to the poor.*
> *He has sent me to proclaim freedom for the prisoners*
> *and recovery of sight for the blind,*
> *to release the oppressed,*
> *to proclaim the year of the Lord's favour.*"
>
> '*Then he rolled up the scroll, gave it back to the attendant and sat down. The eyes of everyone in the synagogue were fastened on him, and he said to them, "Today this scripture is fulfilled in your hearing.*"
>
> *All spoke well of him and were amazed at the gracious words that came from his lips. "Isn't this Joseph's son?" they asked.*' (Luke 4:18–22)

One person who did not understand the message which Jesus was preaching was a Pharisee called Nicodemus. He was a member of the Jewish ruling Council and came to see Jesus at night because he did not want anyone to find out. He realised that Jesus was a special teacher sent by God, because no ordinary person could perform the miracles which Jesus was doing unless God was with him. In reply, Jesus declared to Nicodemus,

> ' "*I tell you the truth, no-one can see the kingdom of God unless he is born again.*"

> *"How can a man be born when he is old?" Nicodemus asked. "Surely he cannot enter a second time into his mother's womb to be born!"*
>
> *Jesus answered, "I tell you the truth, no-one can enter the kingdom of God unless he is born of water and the Spirit.'* (John 3:3–5)

Nicodemus was a wise man searching for the truth. He was deeply puzzled by something very important and took steps to find the answer.

When a child is born, he is 'born of water' (from inside the womb of his mother) and has a physical body and a soul (mind, will and emotions). Inside a child, there is also a human spirit. When a person is born of the Spirit, that spirit becomes alive for the first time. It occurs when a person believes in Jesus Christ's saving power as the Son of God. That person then receives eternal life and so is saved.

> *'For God so loved the world that he gave his one and only Son, so that whoever believes in him shall not perish but have eternal life. For God did not send his Son into the world to condemn the world, but to save the world through him.'* (John 3:16–17)

The 'Good News' is that Jesus came down to earth as a saviour. He came to deal with the problem of our separation from God. By dying on the cross Jesus paid the penalty for our sins.

> *'But God demonstrates his own love for us in this: While we were still sinners, Christ died for us.'* (Romans 5:8)

Jesus came to release us from the burden of guilt and shame and to set us free. At the heart of the gospel are repentance, forgiveness, reconciliation, healing and freedom.

Most people would accept that Jesus Christ existed as a man and that He was put to death on a cross. Fewer people would accept that He rose from the dead and appeared to His disciples on earth. His resurrection from the dead is the key as to whether He was the Son of God. In 1 Corinthians chapter 15, Paul staked everything on the fact of the resurrection.

> *'And if Christ has not been raised, our preaching is useless and so is your faith.'* (1 Corinthians 15:14)

> *'And if Christ has not been raised, your faith is futile; you are still in your sins.'* (1 Corinthians 15:17)

It is fundamental to the gospel to believe that Jesus has been raised from the dead. After the crucifixion the disciples of Jesus were dejected and desolate, but when Jesus reappeared to them having risen from the dead, they changed completely and became confident and bold.

Scholars have spent a great deal of time and effort examining the evidence for the resurrection. Arguments have centred around what happened to Jesus' body after His death on the cross. Is it reasonable to think that it was stolen from the tomb by His disciples, or that the authorities (Jewish or Roman) or Joseph of Arimathea removed it? Could the women who discovered the tomb empty have possibly made a mistake? In his book *Evidence of the Resurrection*, Sir Norman Anderson looks at the facts and invites us to reach a verdict.

We need God and without God we are lost. God gives us an invitation, either to accept or reject Him. Everybody must make a choice (doing nothing is a negative choice). Are you willing to admit that you have fallen short of God's standards and that you need His forgiveness? Do you believe that Christ died on the cross for you and that He rose from the dead? Are you willing to accept Christ as your personal saviour and, by God's grace, to trust and obey Him?

> *'Yet to all who received him, to those who believed in his name, he gave the right to become children of God – children born not of natural descent, nor of human decision or a husband's will, but born of God.'*
>
> (John 1:12–13)

> *'He who has the Son has life; he who does not have the Son of God does not have life.*
>
> *I write these things to you who believe in the name of the Son of God so that you may know you have eternal life.'* (1 John 5:12–13)

The message of the gospel is simple and yet so difficult for many people to accept. Responding to the challenge requires a basic change of attitude.

> *'I tell you the truth, unless you change and become like little children, you will never enter the kingdom of heaven. Therefore, who ever humbles himself like this child is the greatest in the kingdom of heaven. And whoever welcomes a little child like this in my name welcomes me.'*
>
> (Matthew 18:3–5)

Jesus saw the simplicity, humility and trusting nature of children which is reflected in their readiness to learn. Adults find these qualities difficult to retain.

Children are dependent upon their parents for love, care and protection. It is not God's will that they should spend time worrying about food, clothing and shelter. Childhood should be a time of closeness of relationship, a time of joy and vitality, a time for exploration and discovery, a time for learning and correction, a place of openness, freedom, purity and innocence and a place of security free from fear. The world of the adult is so different. How hard it is for him to return to child-like trust. As an earthly father cares for his children and wants the best for them, so does the Heavenly Father with His children.

As we grow up it is easy to forget the simplicity of childhood. The older we become, the more difficult it is to trust naturally. However, whatever our age it is never too late to change the direction of our lives. Remember Nicodemus!

Chapter 2

Obedience

Jesus said:

> *'I have come that they may have life, and have it to the
> full.'*   (John 10:10)

These words are puzzling. Can they be true? The Bible
is often seen as dull and restricting and that it interferes
with personal freedom, thereby preventing the maximum
enjoyment of life. Paradoxically, true freedom comes
from obeying God's rules and following His advice. This
chapter looks at obedience, temptation, disobedience and
discipline.

Teaching children obedience

Two of the most basic needs of a child are love and
discipline. If a child is unable to give and receive love or
is unable to learn obedience, that child will face deep
problems in later life. In infancy, a baby first of all needs
love and attention from his parents and will gradually
begin to show love in return. The security of parental love
is the best environment for parental discipline. Without
love, discipline can become over-harsh. By training, a

child will begin to learn right from wrong and learn to do right. As the child grows older, he will learn that society requires obedience. This benefits both the child and society.

Obedience to teachers makes learning easier, following the doctor's instructions usually leads to better health, policemen and police cars act as reminders to obey the law and judges have power and sanctions to make sure that the law is upheld.

What would happen in a game of football if no one took any notice of the referee? What would happen on the roads if no one took any notice of the Highway Code?

Man's rules have been created to provide order and fairness. Similarly, God's rules were designed for man's well-being. Obedience leads to harmony and peace, dis-obedience leads to discord and conflict.

> *'Whoever loves discipline loves knowledge,*
> *but he who hates correction is stupid.'*
>
> (Proverbs 12:1)

Children need regular training and discipline with constant reminders and love from an early age. Giving a child aged three an ice-cream after he has deliberately misbehaved is bad for the child and is asking for trouble. It may stop the immediate screaming but next time the screaming will be worse if the child does not get what he wants.

A loved and well disciplined child is a happy child.

> *'Discipline your son and he will give you peace;*
> *he will bring delight to your soul.'*   (Proverbs 29:17)

If parents do not provide a combination of love, proper training and discipline for each child, the relationship between parent and child may become strained. Unhealthy tensions often arise and the child may become very difficult to control in the teenage years.

In his old age, Eli must have regretted that he had not disciplined his two sons Hophni and Phinehas properly. God told him, through the child Samuel, that He would punish Eli's family for their wickedness.

> ' "See, I am about to do something in Israel that will make the ears of everyone who hears of it tingle. At that time, I will carry out against Eli everything I spoke against his family – from beginning to end. For I told him that I would judge his family for ever, because of the sin he knew about; his sons made themselves contemptible, and he failed to restrain them. Therefore, I swore to the house of Eli, 'The guilt of Eli's house will never be atoned for by sacrifice or offering.' " '   (1 Samuel 3:11–14)

How did you feel when your parents disciplined you? Were you angry? Did you sulk? Did you complain or did you accept the discipline because you deserved it?

Discipline leads to self-control.

When parents are choosing a school for their child, they usually ask the headmaster what the discipline is like. They want to know whether the children at the school are well-mannered and what sorts of punishments are inflicted when a child misbehaves. The level of discipline will affect the progress of their child.

When children are disobedient, the main responsibility for correction falls on the parents. It is important that children know when they have done wrong, that they recognise it, usually through an apology and that they are punished, if appropriate. Children who learn to apologise when they are young will find it much easier as adults to apologise when they are wrong. Squeezing 'I'm sorry' out of a small child who is stubborn may take time and require patience but the child will learn and may even be grateful to his parents in later life.

As a child must learn obedience, so must a follower of Christ learn obedience to God, obedience to those in authority in the church and obedience to governing authorities.

Obeying God's law

On one occasion in the ministry of Jesus, an expert in the Law tested Jesus with this question:

> ' "Teacher which is the greatest commandment in the Law?'
>
> Jesus replied: " 'Love the Lord your God with all your heart and with all your soul and with all your mind.' This is the first and greatest commandment. And the second is like it: 'Love your neighbour as yourself.' All the Law and the Prophets hang on these two commandments." '
>
> (Matthew 22:36–40)

When Jesus referred to the Law and the Prophets, His audience would have been very familiar with the Old Testament and would have known that Jesus was quoting from the commandment in Deuteronomy 6:4–9 that the Law required total commitment to loving honouring and obeying God. There was no room for compromise.

On another occasion an expert in the Law stood up to test Jesus:

> ' "Teacher," he asked, "what must I do to inherit eternal life?"
>
> "What is written in the Law?" he replied. "How do you read it?"

> *He answered: " 'Love the Lord your God with all your heart and with all your soul and with all your strength and with all your mind'; and, 'Love your neighbour as yourself.' "*
>
> *"You have answered correctly," Jesus replied. "Do this and you will live." '*
>
> *But he wanted to justify himself, so he asked Jesus, "And who is my neighbour?" '* (Luke 10:25–29)

In reply, Jesus told the parable of the Good Samaritan. He wanted the expert in the Law to understand the kind of caring which God is looking for – love that is freely given, love which does not depend upon obligation or merit.

It is hard for us today to imagine the full impact of the parable. There was an attitude of belligerent racism between the Jews and the Samaritans. They hated and despised each other. If a Jew even had a conversation with a Samaritan, he would have been ridiculed or his reputation severely dented. The barriers of prejudice and intolerance were enormous.

It is an uncomfortable parable. The commitment to loving your neighbour as yourself, when it is awkward or dangerous to do so, is a reminder that we should never be complacent.

The problem of the two experts in the Law was that they did not understand that a right relationship with God cannot be built on mere legalism. Keeping rules is not what true faith is all about.

What is our response to God's call for obedience?

How we reply to this question will determine the foundations upon which we are building our lives. If the foundations are well planned, carefully laid and made secure then it will be safe to build on top of them. If the foundations are shaky and unsound there will be trouble later. Having to take down the building and relay the foundations is a painful and costly experience.

> *'Therefore everyone who hears these words of mine and puts them into practice is like a wise man who built his house on the rock. The rain came down, the streams rose, and the winds blew and beat against that house; yet it did not fall, because it had its foundation on the rock. But everyone who hears these words of mine and does not put them into practice is like a foolish man who built his house on sand. The rain came down, the streams rose, and the winds blew and beat against that house, and it fell with a great crash.'* (Matthew 7:24–27)

The good foundation comes from hearing Jesus' words and putting them into practice.

Our attitude to church leaders

Obedience also includes obedience to those in authority in the church.

> *'Obey your leaders and submit to their authority. They keep watch over you as men who must give an account. Obey them so that their work will be a joy, not a burden, for that would be of no advantage to you.'*
>
> (Hebrews 13:17)

God wants us to love and obey our leaders and to submit to them. This does not mean that we should do everything that they say but that we should respect and honour them. Submission means to place yourself under their care, protection and authority. It is a voluntary act of the will.

Leaders, in turn, have an important responsibility to

lead by example. We should want to imitate them. They are like shepherds over a flock of sheep leading them in the right direction and encouraging them. If the sheep become entangled in wire fencing or stray off, the shepherd should lead his sheep back into the fold. A shepherd knows that he cannot force his sheep in a particular direction. Speaking the truth in love and applying correction carefully, where it is needed, is part of a shepherd's task.

Peter, the leader of the twelve apostles, writes to the leaders of the early Church in this way:

> *'Be shepherds of God's flock that is under your care, serving as overseers – not because you must, but because you are willing, as God wants you to be; not greedy for money, but eager to serve; not lording it over those entrusted to you, but being examples to the flock.'*

(1 Peter 5:2–3)

Paul in 1 Timothy chapter 3 sets out the qualities of an overseer – above reproach, the husband of only one wife, temperate, self-controlled, respectable, hospitable, able to teach, not given to much wine, not violent but gentle, not quarrelsome, not a lover of money, able to manage his own family well and to discipline his children, not a recent convert and having a good reputation with outsiders.

The leaders of a church are its pillars and foundations. The purpose of the leaders is to seek the will of God and to establish His kingdom. A healthy church will contain new converts and people at different stages of growth moving towards full maturity. The church will be a place where its people become prepared and equipped for service in the Kingdom of God. It will be where believers are helped to discover their gifts and to develop them to their full potential.

Where there are happy and harmonious relationships amongst the leaders and between leaders and the congregation, God's work is more likely to flourish.

Obeying the law of the land

The Bible also makes it clear that we are all required to obey the law of the land no matter who we are. We are all ambassadors for Christ and need to set a good example especially in today's moral climate. The law of the land is for the benefit of everyone.

> *'Everyone must submit himself to the governing authorities, for there is no authority except that which God has established. The authorities that exist have been established by God.'*   (Romans 13:1)

However, we may face situations where the law of the land conflicts with the word of God. Daniel faced a conflict when King Darius issued a decree that anyone who prayed to any god or man during the following thirty days, except to Darius himself, would be thrown into the lions' den. The decree was irrevocable. Daniel refused to obey the decree and therefore had to take the consequences. God rescued him from the mouth of the lions (Daniel chapter 6). Shadrach, Meshach and Abednego were also rescued by God from the fiery furnace after refusing to obey the command of King Nebuchadnezzar to worship the image of God (Daniel chapter 3). In the New Testament Peter had a miraculous escape from prison (Acts chapter 12).

There are other incidents recorded in the Bible where people have not been rescued. In the Old Testament there were the prophets slaughtered by Jezebel (1 Kings 18:4). In the New Testament John the Baptist was beheaded

(Mark 6:27), Stephen was stoned to death (Acts 7:58–60) and James was put to death by the sword (Acts 12:2). We must therefore be very careful before we deliberately disobey the law of the land and, if we do, we must be willing to accept the consequences for the sake of the gospel.

Temptation and how to resist it

Upon what foundation are you building your life? Is it on the rock or on the sand? What will your attitude be when you are faced with the temptation of pursuing selfish ambition or being 'economical with the truth'? How much do the seven deadly sins feature in your life – anger, envy, gluttony, greed, lust, pride and sloth?

Advertising on the television, in newspapers and magazines exposes us all to temptation. The power of advertising, which exploits the lusts of the eyes (1 John 2:16 AV) leads people to acquire goods and services beyond their needs and resources. Programmes and books about sex and violence are further pressures which are hard to avoid and put wrong ideas into our minds.

It is not wrong to be tempted, the sin lies in falling for the temptation.

There was an occasion in his life when King David could not resist temptation. He lusted after Bathsheba, the wife of Uriah the Hittite, and committed adultery with her. The prophet Nathan confronted David with his sin. David repented and his sin was forgiven but he still had to suffer the consequences (2 Samuel 12). Nathan prophesied that the sword would never depart from his house (verse 10) and out of his own household God would bring calamity upon him (verse 11). It all came true and the details are found in 2 Samuel chapters 13–18.

Jesus Himself was tempted. When He was in the desert for 40 days and nights without food, He was very hungry. He was tempted by the devil three times but He never gave in to temptation.

Firstly, He was tempted to turn stones into bread (Matthew 4:3). He responded by quoting Deuteronomy 8:3:

> 'It is written: "Man does not live on bread alone but on every word that comes from the mouth of the Lord." '

Secondly, the devil took Him to Jerusalem and had Him stand on the highest point of the temple. The devil tempted Him to jump down, whereupon He would be rescued by angels; this would show that He was the Son of God (Matthew 4:5–6).

Jesus responded by quoting Deuteronomy 6:16:

> 'It is also written: "Do not test the Lord your God." '

Thirdly, the devil took Jesus to a very high mountain and showed Him all the kingdoms of the world and their splendour. All these kingdoms would be given to Jesus if He would only bow down and worship the devil (Matthew 4:8–9).

Jesus responded by quoting Deuteronomy 6:13:

> 'For it is written: "Fear the Lord your God, serve him only." '

On each of the three occasions upon which Jesus was tempted, He used the living and active word of God as an effective weapon against the devil and that made Him strong enough to resist the temptation. He went through temptations and therefore knows what it is like when each of us are tempted.

> *'Because he himself suffered when he was tempted, he is able to help those who are being tempted.'*
>
> (Hebrews 2:18)

> *'Therefore, since we have a great high priest who has gone through the heavens, Jesus the Son of God, let us hold firmly to the faith we profess. For we do not have a high priest who is unable to sympathise with our weaknesses, but we have one who has been tempted in every way, just as we are – yet was without sin. Let us then approach the throne of grace with confidence, so that we may receive mercy and find grace to help us in our time of need.'*
>
> (Hebrews 4:14–16)

God's discipline and our response

It is easy to think that a little deliberate sin does not matter and that it will be forgotten. Succumbing to a little temptation leads to bigger temptations. Repenting and confessing our sin and receiving forgiveness from God neutralises the sin but the consequences of the sin do not disappear. Each time we succumb to the temptation we will find it harder to resist the temptation next time. This leads to more mistakes in our lives and makes it harder to keep a close relationship with God. Mistakes can be costly and painful, especially when things do not turn out as we want or expect. God may step in and discipline us for our benefit.

> *' "My son, do not make light of the Lord's discipline,*
> *and do not lose heart when he rebukes you,*

because the Lord disciplines those he loves,
and he punishes everyone he accepts as a son." '

(Hebrews 12:5–6)

'Our fathers disciplined us for a little while as they thought best; but God disciplines us for our good, that we may share in his holiness. No discipline seems pleasant at the time, but painful. Later on, however, it produces a harvest of righteousness and peace for those who have been trained by it.'

(Hebrews 12:10–11)

If unrepented sin builds up inside us, it leads to hardness of heart. Mules are stubborn and need to be broken in. Hardness of heart is part of the old sin nature of man.

Pharaoh was very stubborn when he refused to allow Moses and the Israelites to leave Egypt. It required a series of plagues, each more dreadful that the previous one, to put pressure on Pharaoh to change his mind. It was only when the first born of Pharaoh and all his officials and all the Egyptians as well as the livestock were struck down, that Pharaoh relented. Only the Israelites, who put the sign of the blood of the Passover on their door frames were spared the loss of their first born. Even then, after Moses and the Israelites had fled from Egypt, Pharaoh changed his mind, but it was too late. The story is found in Exodus chapters 7–14.

The Jews were equally stubborn at the time of Jeremiah. They were deliberately and blatantly sinning against the laws of God. Even when Jeremiah prophesied that God would inflict disaster of a most serious kind (a nation to be uprooted torn down and destroyed), if the people did not repent from their wicked ways, they refused to listen.

> ' "Now therefore say to the people of Judah and those living in Jerusalem, 'This is what the LORD says: Look! I am preparing a disaster for you and devising a plan against you. So turn from your evil ways, each one of you, and reform your ways and your actions.' But they will reply, 'It's no use. We will continue with our own plans; each of us will follow the stubbornness of his evil heart.' " '   (Jeremiah 18:11–12)

Are there times when you are stiff-necked and stubborn when you know that what you are doing is wrong? How easy do you find it to admit that you have been wrong? Do you find that you justify wrong actions?

The more stiff-necked and stubborn we are, the greater the discipline God will need to impose to change us. The tougher we are, the more painful the discipline will be. Discipline breaks down hardness of heart. God is the potter and we are like clay. He wants us to be malleable, so that He may make us what He wants us to be.

God wants an undivided heart.

> 'Teach me your way, O LORD,
>   and I will walk in your truth;
> give me an undivided heart,
>   that I may fear your name.'   (Psalm 86:11)

> 'I will give them an undivided heart and put a new spirit in them; I will remove from them their heart of stone and give them a heart of flesh.'   (Ezekiel 11:19)

God longs for us to be obedient so that we may become new people and experience the abundant life which Jesus promised.

Chapter 3

The Kingdom of God

'For the kingdom of God is not a matter of eating and drinking, but of righteousness, peace and joy in the Holy Spirit...'   (Romans 14:17)

The Bible describes the Kingdom of God in a number of different ways but the purpose of this chapter is to explore the intangible qualities of righteousness, peace and joy produced by the Holy Spirit in the life of the Christian.

The Holy Spirit

First, who or what is the Holy Spirit? The Holy Spirit is a person but He is also God. He is the third person of the Trinity, Father, Son and Holy Spirit. We cannot see the Holy Spirit but we can see what He does. What is the Holy Spirit like?

1. He is like a mighty wind, invisible but hugely powerful (Acts 2:2).
2. He is like tongues of fire (Acts 2:3).
3. He is as the breath of life (John 20:22).
4. He is like a dove, sensitive and gentle (Mark 1:10).

The work of the Holy Spirit is to bring power and radiance to the lives of Jesus' followers and to lead them into all truth.

Righteousness

The Kingdom of God is a stark contrast to the materialistic world in which we live. It is not directly concerned with money and possessions but with relationships between ourselves and God and each other. Jesus said,

> *'A person's true life is not made up of the things he owns, no matter how rich he may be.'* (Luke 12:15 GNB)

We are continually making choices for our lives. What are your aims? What are your priorities? Are they following the natural devices and desires of your heart or are they allowing God to change you to be more like Jesus Christ?

Most of us want a mixture of both worlds, but they do not mix. In each of us there is a struggle between the old self and the new nature of Christ born in us when we become Christians. The start to seeking the Kingdom of God is found in Matthew 6:33–34:

> *'But seek first his kingdom and his righteousness and all these things* (food, clothes and drink) *will be given to you as well. Therefore do not worry about tomorrow, for tomorrow will worry about itself. Each day has enough trouble of its own.'*

In the Beatitudes (Matthew 5:3–12) Jesus taught His disciples where true happiness lay. He turned the ideas of the world upside down. It is those who recognise that they are spiritually poor (v. 3) and who learn to depend on God who are truly happy. God is looking for people who are humble, merciful, pure in heart, who set their hearts on righteousness and who are peacemakers. His standards are perfect and point us in the right direction. It is His desire that we should lead lives of righteousness and not be weighted down by sin. Through the death of Jesus on the cross we have been given the bridge to be reconciled with God. This is 'Good News' and we should not be discouraged as we begin the realise how much God wants to change us, albeit gradually. We cannot avoid sin, it is rooted in our nature. What matters is how we respond. We all displease God in our thoughts, words and deeds, in what we ought to have done and in what we ought not to have done.

> *'If we claim to be without sin, we deceive ourselves and the truth is not in us. If we confess our sins, he is faithful and just and will forgive us our sins and purify us from all unrighteousness. If we claim we have not sinned, we make him out to be a liar and his word has no place in our lives.'* (1 John 1:8–10)

God gives us the opportunity to repent so that we can be purified from all unrighteousness. If we confess our sins, God will forgive us. We must do this from our hearts, not just with our lips. Only God knows if we are truly sorry. Dealing with sin can be like dealing with an infected wound. If the wound is cleaned it will heal in time but if it is left untreated it will not heal and the infection may spread. The sooner we deal with the sin the sooner we will feel better.

> *'Repent, then, and turn to God, so that your sins may be wiped out, that times of refreshing may come from the Lord.'* (Acts 3:19)

And yet we often find it so difficult to admit that we have done something wrong or have made a mistake. How does God feel when we deliberately try to justify ourselves when we know in our hearts that what we have said or done is wrong?

Sins are like weeds in the garden. If we regularly tend the garden, feed the soil, water, weed, prune and protect it, flowers, shrubs, vegetables and fruit will flourish. However, if we neglect our gardens, weeds will spring up from nowhere and then multiply. Our gardens will then be unrecognisable. It is much easier to look after a garden regularly little by little than to attack it every few months. Each weed needs to be uprooted thoroughly so that it will die. It is no good pulling up dandelions without the whole of their roots. If left, the roots will grow even stronger than before.

We also need to learn how to forgive others. Sometimes this can be difficult when the other person is not prepared to take responsibility for his wrongdoing and to apologise. However, it is important to be willing to forgive, no matter how hard that may be. Otherwise resentment, bitterness and anger can build-up and fester inside us. We all make mistakes. There will be those times when we need to seek the forgiveness of someone else. We should try and make it easy for that person to forgive us. People do feel better after the forgiveness has taken place.

> *'For if you forgive men when they sin against you, your heavenly Father will also forgive you. But if you do not forgive men their sins, your Father will not forgive your sins.'* (Matthew 6:14–15)

In the parable of the unmerciful servant found in Matthew chapter 18, Jesus tells us to forgive our brothers not seven times but seventy times seven. God has given us the means of being freed from our sins. We need not be locked in fear and guilt.

> *'For sin shall not be your master, because you are not under law, but under grace.'*   (Romans 6:14)

God wants us to have a right relationship not only with Him but also with each other, i.e. in the family, at work, with our friends and neighbours, in our leisure time and at church. Christianity is not simply a matter of personal piety. We should be willing and ready to show a concern for each other, especially when things are not going well.

> *'Carry each other's burdens, and in this way you will fulfil the law of Christ.'*   (Galatians 6:2)

There will always be those who face an extra hard struggle. God has a special concern for these people – the poor, the homeless and the disadvantaged in the world. God never meant that some people should live in luxury whilst others simply struggle to survive. Under the Mosaic law it was part of God's provision that no one (neither the alien, the fatherless nor the widow) went without. After the first gathering of the crops, the farmers were required to leave the surplus for those who were unable to provide for themselves. Things are very different today. While one third of the world has an abundance of food, one third has too little food and one third is starving.

> *'Speak up for those who cannot speak for themselves,*
> *   for the rights of all who are destitute.*
> *Speak up and judge fairly,*
> *   defend the rights of the poor and needy.'*
>
> (Proverbs 31:8–9)

Peace

If we have a right relationship with God and with each other, peace will follow. It will become easier to sense the presence of the Lord.

> *'Who may ascend the hill of the LORD?*
> *Who may stand in his holy place?*
> *He who has clean hands and a pure heart,*
> *who does not lift up his soul to an idol*
> *or swear by what is false.'*   (Psalm 24:3–4)

Coming into the presence of the Lord is a privilege and should not be treated lightly. Beware of the warning in Ecclesiastes:

> *'Guard your steps when you go to the house of God.'*
> (Ecclesiastes 5:1)

Be willing to spend time on your own being still and quiet before God. Learn to put aside the problems which worry you for a few minutes. Think about God and who He is.

> *'Be still, and know that I am God.'*   (Psalm 46:10)

We live in a very noisy and busy world where everybody seems to be rushing about. The pressures of life make it very difficult to be still. The Psalmist encourages us to wait and be patient.

> *'I wait for the LORD, my soul waits,*
> *and in his word I put my hope.*
> *My soul waits for the LORD,*
> *more than watchmen wait for the morning,*
> *more than watchmen wait for the morning.'*
> (Psalm 130:5–6)

'Be still before the Lord *and wait patiently for him.'*
(Psalm 37:7)

Why do we need to be still?

1. Because it is easier to hear. Lying in bed at night you hear many noises that you would not normally hear during the day.
2. Because it is easier to listen. When your mind is full of things it is very difficult to listen. How well you remember something is often a good test of how well you have listened. This is relative because some people have better memories than others.

Psalm 37:7 tells us to be patient. Patience is calm endurance under pain, weariness or provocation. It is a fruit of the Spirit which comes after love, joy, and peace (Galatians 5:22). Be ready to listen and be ready to hear when God speaks.

Finding peace is not always easy.

How do you cope when things do not turn out as you expect? What are you like when faced with a crisis? Do you usually handle it well or badly? Look at the example of Jesus when He knew that He was soon to be arrested, disowned by His disciples, mocked and beaten by guards, brought before Pilate and then crucified. He turned to His Father for help and an angel from heaven appeared to Him and strengthened Him (Luke 22:43).

The French writer, Antoine De Saint-Exupéry was very astute when he wrote:

'L'homme se découvre quand il se mésure avec l'obstacle' – Man only discovers what he is really like when he faces a crisis.

Peace is a gift from God. We need to receive it. We will not receive it by striving. Peace comes from a right relationship with God. It also comes from the renewing of the mind. Only God can renew the mind and will do so if we let Him.

> '*Do not conform any longer to the pattern of this world, but be transformed by the renewing of your mind. Then you will be able to test and approve what God's will is – his good, pleasing and perfect will.*' (Romans 12:2)

If we seek God's will, not ours, then we are more likely to find peace.

Remember:

1. God is the God of knowledge. He knows everything about you, your strengths and your weaknesses, what you are like on the outside and what you are like on the inside. God created you.

2. Peace comes from a revelation of God. We need to ask God for peace – it is part of our inheritance. He is our Father and we are His children. Do not forget that He loved you enough to send His son Jesus to die on the cross for you. That cross is a symbol of peace.

3. Peace comes through prayer. Do you pray for insight for what to do in a difficult situation? King David did.

> '*Show we your ways, O Lord,*
>   *teach me your paths;*
> *guide me in your truth and teach me,*
>   *for you are God my Saviour,*
>   *and my hope is in you all day long.*' (Psalm 25:4–5)

As we meditate on God's word in His presence we will begin to receive inner peace. May we find that the peace of God rules in our hearts.

Joy

Inner peace leads to inner joy. Have you ever gazed upon the Lord?

> *'One thing I ask of the LORD,*
>   *this is what I seek:*
> *that I may dwell in the house of the LORD*
>   *all the days of my life,*
> *to gaze upon the beauty of the LORD*
>   *and to seek him in his temple.'* (Psalm 27:4)

If you gaze upon the beauty of the Lord He will bring you joy. Gazing means looking intently upon. We can become so enwrapped in the presence of the Lord that we forget what lies around and we forget our troubles.

> 'When I look into Your holiness,
> When I gaze into Your loveliness,
> When all things that surround
> Become shadows in the light of You;
> When I've found the joy of reaching Your heart,
> When my will becomes enthralled in Your love,
> When all things that surround
> Become shadows in the light of You:
> I worship You, I worship You,
> The reason I live is to worship You.
> I worship You, I worship You,
> The reason I live is to worship You.'
>
> (© Wayne and Cathy Perrin.
> Used by permission.)

> *'Those who look to him are radiant;*
>   *their faces are never covered with shame.'*
> (Psalm 34:5)

At certain times in our lives we feel close to God; it is then that we will feel the touch of His hand upon our lives and it will cause us to be joyful; we will feel radiant.

Isaiah 60:5 describes the Glory of the Lord:

'Then you will look and be radiant,
your heart will throb and swell with joy.'

God wants us to reflect His glory in this world. When Moses came down from Mount Sinai with the two tablets of testimony in his hands he was not aware that his face was radiant because he had spoken with the Lord. When Aaron and all the Israelites saw that the face of Moses was radiant they were afraid to come near him (Exodus 34:29–30).

The same radiance of the Lord was on Stephen when he was stoned. As he looked up to heaven, full of the Holy Spirit, he saw the Glory of God with Jesus standing at God's right hand (Acts 7:55).

The glory of the New Covenant is described by Paul in 2 Corinthians 3:7–18. The ministry of the Holy Spirit brings righteousness, v. 9. It also transforms our character from within.

'Now the Lord is the Spirit, and where the Spirit of the
Lord is, there is freedom. And we, who with unveiled
faces all reflect the Lord's glory, are being transformed
into his likeness with ever increasing glory, which comes
from the Lord, who is the Spirit.'

(2 Corinthians 3:17–18)

It may be that our glimpses of the glory of the Lord are few and far between. Remember God's promise:

'Come near to God and he will come near to you.'

(James 4:8)

- There is joy which we can experience regularly in our lives.
- There is joy in knowing that we have accepted Jesus Christ as our Lord and Saviour.
- There is joy in repenting and in being made clean.
- There is joy in forgiving and in being forgiven.
- There is joy in loving and in being loved.
- There is joy in giving and in receiving.
- There is joy in serving and in being served.
- There is joy in worshipping God.
- There is joy in reading the Bible.
- There is joy in hearing God speak to us.
- There is joy in realising that God has heard our prayers and has answered them in a way we understand.
- There is joy in obeying God's laws.
- There is joy even in facing trials.

'Consider it pure joy, my brothers, whenever you face trials of many kinds, because you know that the testing of your faith develops perseverance. Perseverance must finish its work so that you may be mature and complete not lacking anything.'　　　　　　　　　　　(James 1:2–4)

Are you building your life desiring food and drink or do you seek righteousness, peace and joy in the Holy Spirit? Our true lives can be hidden from everyone except God. Only He knows.

Chapter 4

The Renewing of the Mind

'Be transformed by the renewing of your mind.'
(Romans 12:2)

Many people have been puzzled by two verses in James chapter 2, namely verses 17 and 26:

'... faith by itself, if it is not accompanied by action, is dead.' (verse 17)

'As the body without the spirit is dead, so faith without deeds is dead.' (verse 26)

In other words, what use is faith if it is not translated into action? Faith and deeds go hand in hand. Faith leads to deeds and deeds build up faith.

Faith is a gift from God but it also comes from the renewing of the mind. This chapter explores how our attitudes may change and how this will affect our actions.

'Therefore, if anyone is in Christ, he is a new creation; the old has gone, and the new has come!'
(2 Corinthians 5:17)

On becoming a Christian a person still has the same body and mind but his spirit is alive. At this moment the renewing of the mind may begin.

> *'You were taught, with regard to your former way of life, to put off your old self, which is being corrupted by its deceitful desires; to be made new in the attitude of your minds; and to put on the new self, created to be like God in true righteousness and holiness.'*
>
> (Ephesians 4:22–24)

When you buy a new car it looks perfect; the paintwork shines and everything about it is clean and bright. After a year the newness and the brightness begin to fade a little. After four or five years the car may begin to show signs of rust. Parts begin to wear out and require replacement. The car is a depreciating asset and one day it will end up in a scrap yard. The opposite is true with our minds. When we become Christians, our old sin nature can be replaced with a new outlook on life. God desires that our minds become newer and newer as we grow as Christians.

> *'Therefore we do not lose heart. Though outwardly we are wasting away, yet inwardly we are being renewed day by day. For our light and momentary troubles are achieving for us an eternal glory that far outweighs them all. So we fix our eyes not on what is seen, but on what is unseen. For what is seen is temporary, but what is unseen is eternal.'* (2 Corinthians 4:16–18)

The Holy Spirit brings freshness to our lives. Jesus said:

> *'Whoever believes in me, as the Scripture has said, streams of living water will flow from within him.'*
>
> (John 7:38)

Is your relationship with God fresh and vibrant, or is it stale and dry? So often our spiritual lives are stagnant. Israel had the same problem in the time of Jeremiah.

> *'My people have committed two sins:*
> *They have forsaken me,*
>   *the spring of living water,*
> *and have dug their own cisterns,*
>   *broken cisterns that cannot hold water.'*

(Jeremiah 2:13)

There is a fundamental difference between a spring of living water and a cistern. A cistern is hewed out of solid stone or made from concrete. Its purpose is to hold water that has been poured into it. At first the water is fresh but as it lies still in the cistern it gradually becomes stale and stagnant. Israel was not very good at building cisterns; they had cracks and leaked. On the other hand the water of a stream is fresh and cool and it flows continuously. It has life in it.

God wants us to tap into the spring of living water daily because there lies its freshness. The same principle applies to food. You can buy tinned food, frozen food, dried food or bottled food, but fresh food is the tastiest. Most fresh food only lasts for a few days but some lasts longer. After that it loses its freshness and becomes stale or goes rotten. There is a huge difference in taste between fresh strawberries and tinned strawberries, fresh plums and bottled plumbs, fresh peas and dried peas, and fresh spinach and frozen spinach. Fresh food cannot be stored for any length of time, we need to go to the shops for it regularly.

It is the same with the word of God. We cannot rely on past experiences too much. We need to spend time daily meditating on the Bible.

In the church and in our fellowship with other believers we have opportunities to hear the word of God. What do you do when you hear a good sermon on a Sunday or have a Bible discussion in a house group which draws you close to God? Do you go away and *'let the word of Christ dwell in you richly'* (Colossians 3:16) or do you forget about it soon afterwards? Our memories retain very little from week to week without encouragement and perseverance.

Sometimes the next step after hearing the word of God should be to open up the Bible at the earliest opportunity and to read it, then to study it, and then to memorise verses. When you have memorised verses you will be able to meditate upon them. Each of us will from time to time hear things that speak to our hearts. The more we take time and effort to read, to study, to memorise, and to meditate, the more our minds will be renewed.

The greatest gift of a teacher is for the pupil to imitate the teacher. To be able to understand the Bible and to meditate upon it and to be able to listen to and hear the voice of God for yourself is pleasing to God and will bring you much peace and joy. You will then be encouraged and want to speak what you have learned to others in the church and to friends and colleagues.

> *'He who refreshes others will himself be refreshed.'*
> (Proverbs 11:25)

In every church the leaders should give the ordinary believer the opportunity to be able to minister. In most churches this opportunity arises in the smaller groups which meet during the week, although there can be opportunities on Sundays.

> *'When you come together, everyone has a hymn, or a word of instruction, a revelation, a tongue or an interpretation.*

All of these must be done for the strengthening of the
church.' (1 Corinthians 14:26)

A healthy church contains a mixture of believers ranging from those who have recently found salvation to those who have been believers for many years. We need to remember that we are all kings and priests and therefore we can all hear from God for ourselves. We need to learn how to do this better.

' ...He has made us to be a kingdom and priests to serve
his God and Father...' (Revelation 1:6)

We are encouraged to minister according to the level of our faith.

'We have different gifts, according to the grace given us. If
a man's gift is prophesying, let him use it in proportion to
his faith. If it is serving, let him serve; if it is teaching, let
him teach; if it is encouraging, let him encourage; if
it is contributing to the needs of others, let him give
generously; if it is leadership, let him govern diligently;
if it is showing mercy, let him do it cheerfully.'

(Romans 12:6–8)

Sometimes we lack confidence.

'Such confidence as this is ours through Christ before God.
Not that we are competent to claim anything for ourselves
but our competence comes from God. He has made us
competent as ministers of a new covenant – not of the
letter but of the Spirit; for the letter kills, but the Spirit
gives life.' (2 Corinthians 3:4–6)

It is very important that where there is freedom to minister in a group situation, everything is done in order (cf 1 Corinthians 14:40). The leader is there not only to lead but to encourage and to stimulate growth. Like children, everyone makes mistakes and we all need to learn from them. We also need to learn to support and love each other.

Worship should also play a vital part in the renewing of our minds. Praising and worshipping God can lift us above the problems of everyday life into His presence. As we reflect on the meaning of the hymns, choruses and songs which we sing we absorb into our hearts words and tunes based on and inspired by the Bible. Praise is to give God the glory for what He has done. He is our Father and Creator, and we should thank Him that he provides for our needs. He is an awesome and wonderful God, loving and just and full of mercy. Worship, in comparison with praise, tends to be quieter and more contemplative giving us the opportunity to draw closer to God in adoration and reverence.

If we study the words of some of the great hymns of the past we can learn a great deal about the minds of the composers. Charles Wesley composed 'And can it be that I should gain', inspired by Ephesians 2:4–5. Isaac Watts composed 'When I survey the wondrous cross' inspired by Galatians 6:14.

In Romans 12:1, Paul urges you to *'offer your bodies as living sacrifices, holy and pleasing to God.'* Sacrifice involves surrender. As you surrender your life to God's will, he will renew your mind and change the way you think. This includes your goals, your values, your attitudes and your priorities. Renewal of the mind is not automatic, it has to be worked at as we all have our natural desires. The choice lies with us.

'Those who live according to the sinful nature have their minds set on what that nature desires; but those who live

in accordance with the Spirit have their minds set on what the Spirit desires. The mind of sinful man is death, but the mind controlled by the Spirit is life and peace; the sinful mind is hostile to God. It does not submit to God's law, nor can it do so. Those controlled by the sinful nature cannot please God.' (Romans 8:5–8)

As your mind begins to change you will experience the things that God has planned for your life. God will not reveal His plans or His secrets to a mind which is at enmity with Him. The blessings of God come from discovering God's will for your life. Paul describes this as *'... his good, pleasing and perfect will'* (Romans 12:2).

Chapter 5

Wisdom and Truth

Wisdom

> 'Wisdom brightens a man's face
>   and changes its hard appearance.'   (Ecclesiastes 8:1)

> 'The truth will set you free.'   (John 8:32)

After King David had died, God appeared to Solomon in a dream and asked him what he wished for most as a gift. Solomon asked for a discerning heart to govern and to distinguish between right and wrong. God was pleased with Solomon and not only promised him a wise and discerning heart but also riches and honour and a long life, provided he obeyed God's commands and statutes.

Sadly, we know that King Solomon did not always walk in God's ways nor did he continue to obey His statutes and commands. In the book of Ecclesiastes Solomon reflects on his life and gives advice.

If God were to ask you what you wished for most would you have chosen wisdom? This chapter looks at wisdom and truth and their benefits.

What are the things in your life which bring contentment and which of them have a lasting value? What are the things in your life which bring security?

Solomon obtained everything a man could desire and yet he was unhappy in his old age. He came to realise that there is more security in knowing God than in the transitory things of life.

> *'Wisdom is a shelter*
>   *as money is a shelter,*
> *but the advantage of knowledge is this:*
>   *that wisdom preserves the life of its possessor.'*
>
> (Ecclesiastes 7:12)

Wisdom is the ability to use information and knowledge well to solve problems – finding the best alternative – skill in living. Wisdom is not being intellectual. Wisdom is what the biblically orientated man would do in the circumstances.

In 1 Kings 3:16–27 two women came before Solomon for a ruling. Both of them had given birth but one of the babies had died during the night. A dispute had arisen as to which of them was the true mother of the living baby. Solomon listened to both of them and gave his ruling.

> *'When all Israel heard the verdict the king had given, they held the king in awe, because they saw that he had wisdom from God to administer justice.'*
>
> (1 Kings 3:28)

Solomon's fame spread far and wide and he wrote three thousand proverbs, the best of which are contained in the book of Proverbs. The wisdom of Solomon is expressed in short sharp sayings which cover all aspects of life, from the training of children to old age. There are proverbs on family life, work, money, how to make decisions, how to behave, act and think.

'The fear of the LORD *is the beginning of wisdom.'*
(Proverbs 9:10)

'The fear of the LORD *is the beginning of knowledge,*
but fools despise wisdom and discipline.'
(Proverbs 1:7)

'My son, pay attention to what I say;
listen closely to my words.
Do not let them out of your sight,
keep them within your heart;
for they are life to those who find them
and health to a man's whole body.
Above all else, guard your heart,
for it is the wellspring of life.' (Proverbs 4:20–23)

In the New Testament Paul writes about the difference between worldly wisdom and life in Christ where the real wisdom lies.

'For the message of the cross is foolishness to those who are perishing, but to us who are being saved it is the power of God. For it is written:
"I will destroy the wisdom of the wise;
the intelligence of the intelligent I will frustrate."'
(1 Corinthians 1:18–19)

'It is because of him that you are in Christ Jesus, who has become for us wisdom from God – that is, our right-eousness, holiness and redemption.'
(1 Corinthians 1:30)

Reading the Bible and meditating upon its words will bring you insight and understanding and the ability to solve problems. Your thought pattern will change.

Truth

The amount of light there is determines how we see things. A shaft of bright sunlight beaming into a dark room reveals that the air is full of dust. Colours can appear different under natural and artificial light. The brighter the light the more noticeable are dirty spots, stains, marks and cobwebs. Our minds also see things in different lights.

Jesus said:

> *'I am the light of the world. Whoever follows me will never walk in darkness, but will have the light of life.'*
> (John 8:12)

Jesus emphasised the difference between light and darkness. His life was a shining example of a new way to live. He challenges us to live in the light and to follow Him in goodness, righteousness and truth. When we are in the light we will be able to see the way forward and not stumble in the darkness.

> *'For God, who said, "Let light shine out of darkness," made his light shine in our hearts to give us the light of the knowledge of the glory of God in the face of Christ.'*
> (2 Corinthians 4:6)

Living in the light means telling the truth. The opposite of truth is lying and this includes the half truth, the little white lie, distortion, reckless words, breaking promises and leaving out part of the truth to create a wrong or false impression. Once words have been said they cannot be taken back. Words are like toothpaste, they come out easily and you can never take them back again.

> *'He who guards his mouth and his tongue*
> *keeps himself from calamity.'*   (Proverbs 21:23)

In English Civil Law evidence before a court is often given in the form of an affidavit – a statement on oath. The plaintiff or the defendant signs his name to the document and then swears on the Bible by saying:

> 'I swear by Almighty God, that this is my name and handwriting, and that the contents of this my affidavit are true.'

Similarly before a witness gives evidence in a Criminal Court of Law a defendant takes the Bible in his right hand and says:

> 'I swear by Almighty God that the evidence I shall give will be the truth, the whole truth and nothing but the truth.'

The alternative to swearing on the Bible is to affirm the truth.

A false statement in an affidavit is a criminal offence which can lead to prosecution, and false evidence given on oath in a court of law is perjury which can lead to a prison sentence for contempt of court. It is because the truth has been devalued in society that such legislation exists. And yet swearing an oath on the Bible is inconsistent with the teaching of Jesus.

> ' "Again, you have heard that it was said to the people long ago, 'Do not break your oath, but keep the oaths you have made to the Lord.' But I tell you, Do not swear at all: either by heaven, for it is God's throne; or by the earth, for it is his footstool; or by Jerusalem, for it is the city of the*

*Great King. And do not swear by your head, for you
cannot make even one hair white or black. Simply let your
'Yes' be 'Yes', and your 'No', 'No'; anything beyond this
comes from the evil one.'' '* (Matthew 5:33–37)

Look at the lack of truth in the life of Jacob and his
relatives. Genesis chapters 27–33 describe how trickery
and deceit caused bad family relationships.

Jacob tricked his father Isaac, who was old and blind,
into giving the blessing of the birthright of the eldest son
to him rather than to his elder twin brother Esau. Jacob
stole the special inheritance from Esau. His mother,
Rebecca, cunningly helped him to do it. Jacob then fled
in fear of his life to his Uncle Laban in Haran, never to see
his mother again (Genesis chapter 27).

Later on Laban deceived Jacob. He promised Jacob that
in return for working for him for seven years, Jacob could
marry his younger daughter Rachel. Laban tricked Jacob
into marrying his elder daughter Leah and then made
him work a further seven years for Rachel making a total
of fourteen years (Genesis chapter 29).

Laban was also dishonest over the payment of wages to
Jacob. When it was time to agree payment, Jacob asked
that instead of wages he should receive all the black
spotted and speckled sheep from among the flocks of
Laban; Laban agreed but the same day he removed all the
black spotted and speckled sheep from his flocks (Genesis
chapter 30). It is hardly surprising that Jacob should
accuse Laban of cheating and changing his wages ten
times (cf Genesis 31:7).

The dishonesty in the family lay in Rachel too. When
Jacob left Laban, he took his family and his possessions
with him. When Laban had gone out to shear his sheep,
Rachel stole her father's household gods. When Laban
caught up with Rachel and searched her tent she deceived

him. Her silence distorted the truth. Moreover Jacob deceived Laban by not telling him that he was running away (Genesis chapter 31).

On a happier note after twenty years of separation Jacob returned home to meet his brother Esau. Jacob was in great fear and distress as to how his twin-brother would react and could not sleep the night before he was due to meet him. He thought that the best way to be reconciled was to give his twin-brother a large gift. Esau did not want Jacob's possessions but to be at peace with his brother (Genesis chapters 32 and 33).

Failure to tell the truth was infectious and caused a great deal of unhappiness for Isaac, Rebecca, Esau, Jacob, Laban, Leah and Rachel, as well as for many others.

God must be sad to see how much the truth is distorted today. We have learned to distort it both secretly and openly and in subtle ways. We must recognise deceit and lies and take steps to put things right.

Inside each of us is our conscience which distinguishes right from wrong. It is close to our heart. If we listen to our conscience it will influence our thoughts and conduct. If we choose not to take notice of our conscience it will have less influence on us and our selfish nature will become stronger and take over. At first there may be no outward difference in our nature, but sooner or later we will give ourselves away. Eventually, our conscience, if un-protected, will become insensitive and ineffective.

King Ahab had a very weak conscience. With the scheming of his wife Queen Jezebel, he used his power and influence to steal Naboth's vineyard. She arranged for Naboth to be stoned to death. However, things did not turn out as Ahab expected. When the prophet Elijah told Ahab that he was going to be punished for his greed, Ahab was petrified. The king changed out of his expensive robes and sought God's mercy by putting on sackcloth and fasted. God did, in fact, show mercy to Ahab and he lived a further three years before he was killed in battle. However, his sons, when they became king in turn, died young. Jezebel, who showed no remorse for her actions, died a terrible death by being thrown from the top of the palace and her body being eaten by wild dogs. The story of Naboth's vineyard is found in 1 Kings chapter 21. It teaches us that God sees everything and God is a just judge.

The armour of God

Standing up for the truth is not easy because there is so much darkness around. The armour of God is to keep us strong and to provide protection from the darts and arrows of life.

> *'Therefore put on the full armour of God, so that when the day of evil comes, you may be able to stand your ground, and after you have done everything, to stand.'*
> (Ephesians 6:13)

Do you use the armour of God? Do you put on all the armour of God? Armour is only as strong as its weakest point and you will not know where the darts and arrows of life will pierce.

> *'Stand firm then, with the **belt of truth** buckled round your waist.'* (Ephesians 6:14)

How resolute are you when faced with an issue about the truth? How loyal are you to the truth when placed in an awkward position?

*'With the **breastplate of righteousness** in place.'*
(Ephesians 6:14)

Do you hunger and thirst after righteousness? (Matthew 5:6).

Do you seek to act justly, and to love mercy and to walk humbly with your God? (Micah 6:8).

Beware of the warning in Ecclesiastes 7:16:

> *'Do not be over-righteous,*
> *neither be over-wise...'*

> *'And with your feet fitted with the readiness that comes from the **gospel of peace**.'*
> (Ephesians 6:15)

Are you ready and willing to talk about the gospel to others?

> *'He who wins souls is wise.'*
> (Proverbs 11:30)

How much difference has the gospel made to your life? How much concern does it cause you that some of your relatives, friends and colleagues may miss eternal life? If you find it difficult to talk about the gospel, have you considered quoting a proverb from the Bible to an unbeliever? Proverbs are not so threatening and often produce a good reaction; they can act as an introduction.

> *'In addition to all this, take up the **shield of faith**, with which you can extinguish all the flaming arrows of the evil one.'*
> (Ephesians 6:16)

In whom is your faith placed? Where does your faith come from? (cf Romans 10:17). How is your faith affected when things do not turn out as you expect? Are you easily discouraged?

*'Take the **helmet of salvation**.'* (Ephesians 6:17)

Do you have the assurance of eternal security? Are you thankful that you have been saved? If you have doubts, how well do you cope with them and do you seek help?

*'And the **sword of the Spirit** which is the word of God.'*
(Ephesians 6:17)

How well do you know the Bible? Do you memorise and meditate on verses? Do you study the Bible regularly? Do you bring it into everyday conversation? Does it bring peace and joy to your heart as you read it?

'Dear friend, I pray that you may enjoy good health and that all may go well with you, even as your soul is getting along well. It gave me great joy to have some brothers come and tell about your faithfulness to the truth and how you continue to walk in the truth. I have no greater joy than to hear that my children are walking in the truth.' (3 John 2–4)

Walking in the truth promotes good health and is essential for spreading the gospel. Failure to do so is a stumbling block to good relationships and will lead to a lack of trust and insecurity.

'Do your best to present yourself to God as one approved, a workman who does not need to be ashamed and who correctly handles the word of truth.' (2 Timothy 2:15)

Chapter 6

Health, Healing and Wholeness

'Reckless words pierce like a sword,
but the tongue of the wise brings healing.'

(Proverbs 12:18)

Healing is an emotive word in the Church. Denominations vary enormously in how they handle this sensitive area. Those churches seeking 'spiritual renewal' take a very positive and active approach in claiming that the exhortations made by Paul are still applicable today.

'Follow the way of love and eagerly desire spiritual
gifts, especially the gift of prophecy.'

(1 Corinthians 14:1)

However, the traditional churches lay much more emphasis on the fruit of the Spirit, as described by Paul in Galatians 5:22–23: *'love, joy, peace, patience, kindness, goodness, faithfulness, gentleness and self-control.'* It is a more patient approach for the spiritual, mental and emotional well-being of the believer.

Both approaches have much to offer but each can learn from the other. The person exercising a spiritual gift will be more productive if the fruit of the Spirit abounds in his life. Similarly, the person whose nature is controlled by the fruit of the Spirit will be more productive if he uses the gifts of the Spirit which God has given him. This chapter seeks to provide a foundation for healthy living.

The Bible teaches that there is more to man than just body and soul. The body is the physical side of man; the soul is made up of the mind (how we think), the will (what we want) and the emotions (how we feel and this includes the conscience). Inside a man there is also a human spirit. Until a person is 'born again' his spirit is inactive, i.e. it has no influence on the workings of his mind, will and emotions – his soul runs his life. When a person is 'born again' his human spirit becomes alive. The spirit of God (the Holy Spirit) comes into his life and makes him different.

> *'Therefore, if anyone is in Christ, he is a new creation; the old has gone, the new has come!'*
>
> (2 Corinthians 5:17)

The Holy Spirit is very powerful and can change the way a person thinks, acts and feels. The Holy Spirit has different priorities which can conflict with a person's natural desires. The more a person allows the Holy Spirit to influence his soul, the greater the change will be. Each of us needs to examine ourselves carefully and thoroughly to discover what we are like on the inside. Are we soft and malleable like clay so that the Holy Spirit can mould us into a shape pleasing to God, or are we tough and hard making change much more difficult? The choice lies with us.

The following questions will give you an indication as to the state of your health:

Are you healthy in body?

1. Do you take regular physical exercise? Are you reasonably fit?
2. Do you eat fresh food and have a balanced diet? Are you overweight, underweight or of average weight?
3. Do you make time to relax, to pursue hobbies, and do you take holidays?
4. Do you allow sufficient time to sleep?
5. Do you take time to be still and quiet?
6. Do you look after yourself?

Are you healthy in soul?

1. Do you have good relationships at home, in your place of work, in the church and in other areas of your life?
2. Do you find it easy or difficult to show and receive love?
3. Do you find it easy or difficult to make friends?
4. Are you selfish or do you think of others?
5. Are you generous or mean with your time, possessions and money?
6. Do you find it easy or difficult to admit that you are wrong sometimes? Do you find it easy or difficult to apologise?
7. Do you find it easy or difficult to forgive and be forgiven?
8. Do you find it easy or difficult to listen to and understand others?
9. Do you become angry easily? Do you show self-control?
10. How much notice do you take of your conscience?

Are you healthy in spirit?

1. Do you read the Bible regularly and meditate upon it?
2. Do you spend times in prayer with God, alone and with others?
3. Are you honest with God?
4. Are you regularly committed to a church?
5. Are you able to listen to the voice of God?
6. What are your priorities in life? Psalm 84:1–2 and 10.
7. Are you being transformed by the renewing of your mind? (Romans 12.2).
8. Do you make every effort to live in peace with all men and to be holy? (Hebrews 12.14).
9. Are you happy to serve and be served?

These questions may seem obvious but the answers will give a guide to the state of your health.

Jesus Christ was strong physically, emotionally and spiritually and was the person most able to cope with the stresses and strains of life. He faced enormous pressures far beyond the pressures we face or bare. He came to bear our stresses and burdens too.

> 'Surely he took up our infirmities
>   and carried our sorrows,
> yet we considered him stricken by God,
>   smitten by him, and afflicted.
> But he was pierced for our transgressions,
>   he was crushed for our iniquities,
> the punishment that brought us peace was upon him,
>   and by his wounds we are healed.'   (Isaiah 53:4–5)

How does the spiritual man deal with his problems?

* **In the body**: by recognising sickness and stress, by seeking medical and other help, by resting, by changing his diet and by exercising.

- **In the soul**: by learning to repent and forgive, to receive and give love and to show the fruit of the Spirit, *'love, joy, peace, patience, kindness, goodness, faithfulness, gentleness and self-control'* (Galatians 5:22).
- **In the spirit**: by praying and worshipping and making every effort to be holy; reading the Bible; being part of the church in the local community and making a contribution to it; by seeking to be continually filled with the Holy Spirit.

The Church is full of sinners who have repented of their sins and who need the encouragement of being part of the Body of Christ. Having got this far, each of us will have realised that there is much that is wrong in our lives, but there is a foundation upon which to build. Just like those outside the Church, we all have problems, some of which are deeply rooted in our personalities. Some have arisen through our upbringing and some through our own choices in life. God can use our weaknesses as well as our strengths.

Health improves through following the word of God, believing what it says and obeying it. Our repentance, assurance of forgiveness and our forgiveness of others are part of the process of healing. They are not signs of weakness but of strength – although the world may dispute this.

It is healthy to get to know yourself and to begin to recognise your faults and good points.

'For by the grace given me I say to every one of you: Do not think of yourself more highly than you ought, but rather think of yourself with sober judgment, in accordance with the measure of faith God has given you.' (Romans 12:3)

'If anyone thinks he is something when he is nothing, he deceives himself. Each one should test his own actions.

Then he can take pride in himself, without comparing himself to somebody else, for each one should carry his own load.' (Galatians 6:3–5)

Obey the truth.

'Surely you desire truth in the inner parts;
you teach me wisdom in the inmost place.'

(Psalm 51:6)

Pursue righteousness.

We should not forget that there is a continuous battle in our hearts between the new nature (the mind of Christ) and our old sin nature. The prophet Jeremiah reminds us:

'The heart is deceitful above all things and beyond cure.
Who can understand it?' (Jeremiah 17:9)

In trying to follow in the footsteps of Jesus Christ we will fail when we rely on our own strength, but the more we follow in His footsteps the closer we will draw near to Him and the more we will live like Him. Release of many of our problems comes through repentance and forgiveness. Then there is love. We may be spiritual giants exercising all the spiritual gifts but if we do not have love then they are all in vain. Love is paramount – the most important fruit and gift of the Spirit.

'Love is patient, love is kind. It does not envy, it does not boast, it is not proud. It is not rude, it is not self-seeking, it is not easily angered, it keeps no record of wrongs. Love does not delight in evil but rejoices with the truth. It always protects, always trusts, always hopes, always perseveres.' (1 Corinthians 13:4–7)

Love encompasses serving. It enables us to lose our self-importance and to do some of the least attractive tasks in the church.

At the time of Jesus, washing the dirty, hot and smelly feet before a meal was the task of a servant. So at a meal shortly before the Passover feast when Jesus got up to wash the feet of his disciples, there must have been an air of shock, shame and embarrassment. How could their very important leader who performed miracles, calmed a storm and fed a crowd of 5000 people, stoop to wash their feet! Peter objected most strongly until he realised that Jesus was showing that He loved and cared for His disciples and that He was setting an example.

Jesus said:

> *'Now that I, your Lord and Teacher, have washed your feet, you also should wash one another's feet. I have set you an example that you should do as I have done for you. I tell you the truth, no servant is greater than his master, nor is a messenger greater than the one who sent him. Now that you know these things, you will be blessed if you do them.'* (John 13:14–17)

We too should follow the example of Jesus to show our love and commitment to our church. Serving brings fulfilment and helps you forget your own problems. It makes you feel better. Jesus wants everyone in the church to be like servants. We should also learn to encourage each other.

> *'Let us not give up meeting together, as some are in the habit of doing, but let us encourage one another.'* (Hebrews 10:25)

The miraculous gift of healing

God chooses whom He heals. We can ask quietly on our own, or in a group or go to the church leaders for prayer. We can go to a person who has a ministry in healing but it is only God who heals. God does perform miracles and the Church should not limit His power. At the same time we must learn to accept the will of God. As we pray, or others pray on our behalf, faith is put to the test, to believe that God knows what is best for us even though it may not be what we expect or immediately wish. In these pressurised situations it can be hard to discern God's will especially when there seems to be no response. It is therefore very important to be really open to allow the Holy Spirit to move freely inside us. There are many things which we do not understand. There can even be healing in accepting the difficult position we are in, however hard that may be, and this will lead to peace and relaxation in one's whole body.

The Bible lists the spiritual gifts for the common good:

> '... the message of wisdom ... the message of knowledge ... faith ... gifts of healing ... miraculous powers ... prophecy ... distinguishing between spirits ... speaking in different kinds of tongues ... the interpretation of tongues.' (1 Corinthians 12:8–10)

All these spiritual gifts are used in the ministries of healing and deliverance. For instance, through a message of knowledge, those ministering may receive details of a person's problem or illness. There are prophecies that healing will take place. God expects those endowed with such gifts to use them wisely. Be open to the use of spiritual gifts and listen to what is said. Test it, see if a prophecy comes true in time. Do not forget about it. Hold it in your heart. Be encouraged if it comes true and be thankful to God.

What happens if someone who has been prayed for is not healed? How is that dealt with in relation to biblical truth? Those with healing ministries tend to assume that people will be healed. God expects us to have faith but there is a danger in being over zealous which can lead to disappointment, resentment and bitterness.

God does not expect us to go beyond the level of our faith. For most Christians, growth is gradual. If a person is dying from cancer it may be right to pray for physical healing but that is a big prayer. So often God wants us to get used to praying for the little things first. Care and sensitivity are needed in our choice of words. There can be healing of the body without dealing with emotional or spiritual problems. Equally, a physical handicap or illness may remain untouched, whilst that person begins to see God in a new and different light leading to both emotional and spiritual healing. God can use pain and suffering to draw people close to Him, to challenge their direction and priorities in life. Jesus had a much wider and deeper vision of healing than we do. He came to heal the sick in body, soul and spirit.

It is often forgotten by Christians that our bodies, even before we are fully grown, have started to deteriorate. There is a natural and irreversible decaying process as we grow older.

> 'For the creation was subjected to frustration, not by its own choice, but by the will of the one who subjected it, in hope that the creation itself will be liberated from its bondage to decay and brought into the glorious freedom of the children of God.' (Romans 8:20–21)

This is a depressing thought but we should not lose heart.

> *'Therefore we do not lose heart. Though outwardly we are wasting away, yet inwardly we are being renewed day by day. For our light and momentary troubles are achieving for us an eternal glory that far outweighs them all. So we fix our eyes not on what is seen, but on what is unseen. For what is seen is temporary, but what is unseen is eternal.'* (2 Corinthians 4:16–18)

Even Paul had a thorn in the flesh which was not removed even though he pleaded to God three times for it to be taken away (2 Corinthians 12:7–10).

No-one goes through life without some form of sickness or disease. Many illnesses are minor and after a short period of time recovery usually takes place. This is what we expect. It is when recovery does not come that help is needed. Similarly it is part of life for each of us to face a huge variety of problems. Sometimes they are too big for us to deal with on our own. Help is needed. The Church is in a unique position to provide this help. It is commonplace for people to have bad backs or pains in the neck and shoulders. The cause may be physical, a deformity from birth or bad posture, or it may be emotional through tension and worry. Another alternative is the person may be affected by evil spirits and/or afflicted by something from the past which may be difficult to discern. A wise counsellor looks at the whole person, body, soul and spirit. The symptoms may have existed for a short or long time. They may have been hidden under the surface and have suddenly come to light in a crisis. Each of us is a human being and it is important not to address only a spiritual problem when it may be a deep physical, mental or emotional problem.

Most healing is gradual. For most of the time help is needed to put a sick person into a position where he is able to receive God's touch towards wholeness. Be sensitive to the Holy Spirit but be realistic in exercising the spiritual gifts which God has given you. It is a big responsibility. Remember...

  'Reckless words pierce like a sword,
    but the tongue of the wise brings healing.'

(Proverbs 12:18)

Chapter 7

Spiritual Growth

'But grow in the grace and knowledge of our Lord and Saviour Jesus Christ.'   (2 Peter 3:18)

Spiritual growth begins at the point of salvation. God desires that from being like new-born babies, we grow into mature spiritual men and women capable of dealing with the problems of life in a wise and disciplined way.

Why do so many 'born again' men and women never reach maturity?

'When I was a child, I talked like a child, I thought like a child, I reasoned like a child. When I became a man, I put childish ways behind me.'   (1 Corinthians 13:11)

It is considered a little odd when adults retain childish ways and it may seem a little odd to God when believers never go beyond the elementary teachings about Christ (Hebrews 6:1–2).

If an acorn remains an acorn all its life and does not develop into an oak tree its main purpose has been lost. Of the thousands and thousands of acorns which fall to the ground each year, only a small proportion germinate and fewer still grow into large oak trees. This chapter examines how we may grow spiritually and how God may assess our lives.

Are you storing things in a garage or attic – books, blankets, clothes etc? Generally, the longer they are left in storage the less use they are. Books gather dust and some become out of date as new editions appear. Blankets may get eaten by moths and clothes generally fade and some may go out of fashion. Sadly, many Bibles gather dust on book shelves for long periods of time. Where is your Bible? How often do you open it and read it? Do you allow what it says to affect the way you think and act?

As we participate in the church we may listen to many good sermons and attend a few conferences or house parties where we are uplifted. Some of us will take notes and then file them away and forget about them. Weeks, months or years later, we may come across them again and wonder what to do with them. It can be both rewarding and refreshing to look through the old notes every so often to remind ourselves what we were taught as spiritual babes and children. Unless we apply the truths which we have learned they will be of no use. If we do apply them we will grow.

The potential for growth is enormous.

> 'Again Jesus said, "What shall we say the kingdom of God is like, or what parable shall we use to describe it? It is like a mustard seed, which is the smallest seed you plant in the ground. Yet when planted, it grows and becomes the largest of all garden plants, with such big branches that the birds of the air can perch in its shade."'
> (Mark 4:30–32)

Healthy and strong roots are essential for growth and roots need the right kind of soil. Heathers, gorse and rhododendrons require an acid soil base whereas roses require an alkali soil base. Many plants and shrubs like a neutral soil base. If heather is planted in a alkali soil base it may survive but it will always struggle, unless steps are taken to change the base of the soil such as adding peat which builds up the level of acidity. Roses will struggle in an acid soil base. Some plants, e.g. geraniums like soil which drains easily and some plants, e.g. cacti flourish even when neglected in poor soil and with very little water. Plants need the right conditions for growth and so do human beings.

Jesus taught that the Kingdom of God is within you (cf Luke 17:21). Are the conditions right to allow the seed within you to grow?

> *'Like newborn babies, crave pure spiritual milk, so that by it you may grow up in your salvation, now that you have tasted that the Lord is good.'* (1 Peter 2:2)

It is curious that the elementary teachings about Christ found in Hebrews chapter 6:1–2 are not more widely known – repentance, faith, baptism, the laying on of hands, the resurrection of the dead and eternal judgment. Would you be able to explain these elementary teachings to an unbeliever?

Repentance from acts that lead to death

Repentance can be defined as the acknowledgement with sorrow of all personal sin and the willingness to turn away from it.

Right at the beginning of their ministries both John the Baptist (Matthew 3:1–2) and Jesus (Matthew 4:17) preached *'Repent, for the kingdom of heaven is near.'*

One person who repented of his sins after he met Jesus was Zacchaeus the tax collector. The people living in

Jericho must have been amazed how a wealthy chief tax collector should decide to give half his possessions to the poor and pay back anybody whom he had cheated of anything four times the amount (Luke 19:1–10).

The need to repent does not cease upon salvation. The need to repent runs throughout life.

Faith in God

In the AV Hebrews 11:1 faith is defined as *'the substance of things hoped for, the evidence of things not seen.'* The substance is the promises of God.

> *'So then faith cometh by hearing, and hearing by the word of God.'*
> (Romans 10:17 AV)

It is as we read the Bible, study it and meditate upon its words that our faith will grow. Faith is learning to trust God. The words of Jesus inspire faith for salvation and for our walk with God.

> *'But without faith it is impossible to please him.'*
> (Hebrews 11:6 AV)

Instructions about baptism

There are four main baptisms recorded in the Bible:
- **Baptism into the Body** – This occurs at conversion. When a person gives his life to Christ, the Holy Spirit enters the life of that person (1 Corinthians 12:12–14).
- **Baptism in water** – The public declaration to the world and the devil that a person identifies with the death of Jesus Christ on the cross, his burial in

the tomb and his resurrection from the dead (1 Peter 3:21).

- **Baptism of the Holy Spirit** – *'To be clothed with power from on high'* (Luke 24:49).
- **Baptism with fire** – for refining and purification (Matthew 3:11–12).

The laying on of hands

When one person lays his hands upon another for a spiritual purpose:
- To transfer leadership (Numbers 27:18 and 22–23).
- To impart wisdom (Deuteronomy 34:9).
- To impart blessing (Matthew 19:13–15).
- To impart healing (Luke 4:40).
- To impart the Holy Spirit (Acts 8:16–17).
- To commission people for a specific task, e.g. evangelism (Acts 13:2–3).
- To impart a spiritual gift (1 Timothy 4:14).

Note the warning in 1 Timothy 5:22:

> *'Do not be hasty in the laying on of hands, and do not share in the sins of others. Keep yourself pure.'*

The resurrection of the dead

Death is not the end. There are frequent references in the New Testament to resurrection in the last days. Jesus himself stated:

> *'Do not be amazed at this, for a time is coming when all who are in their graves will hear his voice and come out – those who have done good will rise to live, and those who have done evil will rise to be condemned.'*
>
> (John 5:28–29)

There is the picture in Philippians 3:20–21 that the righteous will receive glorified bodies at the time of their resurrection.

> *'But our citizenship is in heaven. And we eagerly await a Saviour from there, the Lord Jesus Christ, who, by the power that enables him to bring everything under his control, will transform our lowly bodies so that they will be like his glorious body.'*

Shortly after this will be the judgment.

The eternal judgment

The Bible makes it clear that each person, whether a believer or unbeliever, is accountable to God. This means that the whole world must face a time of judgment.

For we will all stand before God's judgment seat.

> *'It is written:*
>
> *" 'As surely as I live,' says the Lord,*
> *'Every knee will bow before me,*
> *   every tongue will confess to God.' "*
>
> *So then, each of us will give an account of himself to God.'*   (Romans 14:10–12)

For the believer it will be shortly after he has received his heavenly body that he will appear before the judgment seat of Christ.

> *'For we must all appear before the judgment seat of Christ, that each one may receive what is due to him for the things done while in the body whether good or bad (worthless).'*   (2 Corinthians 5:10)

75

It is not a judgment of condemnation (Romans 8:1) but a judgment to assess rewards. The true believer will be judged not in respect of righteousness but in respect of service rendered to Christ in proportion to the talents he has been given.

On the day of judgment our works as Christians will be judged. God will look at our lives and at what we have done, having been given Jesus Christ as the foundation upon which to build.

> *'By the grace God has given me, I laid a foundation as an expert builder, and someone else is building on it. But each one should be careful how he builds. For no-one can lay any foundation other than the one already laid, which is Jesus Christ. If any man builds on this foundation using gold, silver, costly stones, wood, hay or straw, his work will be shown for what it is, because the Day will bring it to light. It will be revealed with fire, and the fire will test the quality of each man's work. If what he has built survives, he will receive his reward. If it is burned up, he will suffer loss; he himself will be saved, but only as one escaping through the flames.'*
>
> (1 Corinthians 3:10–15)

On the day of judgment there may be a few surprises. God looks on the inside and not on the outward appearance. He knows our motives and how obedient we have been. Quality is more important than quantity. There will be those who have been building steadily throughout their lives with whom God will be pleased. There will be others whose works appear to have stored up treasures in heaven, but after the fire very little will remain.

The nature of the reward is not mentioned in 1 Corinthians chapter 3 but other passages indicate that the reward may be in the form of crowns.

We are exhorted to run the race to get a crown which will last forever (1 Corinthians 9:25).

There is a crown of rejoicing for those who long for his coming (1 Thessalonians 2:19).

There is the crown of life for those who have persevered under trial and have stood the test and loved Him (James 1:12).

There is a crown of glory which will never fade away for the good shepherds of God's flock (1 Peter 5:4).

There is a crown of life for those who are faithful to the point of death (Revelation 2:10).

Revelation chapter 4 seems to indicate that those who have been rewarded with crowns will lay them before the throne of heaven as an act of worship. Thinking about the different types of crowns will give us an understanding as to what is important to God.

Then there will be those who do not receive a crown at all and this will lead to a sense of shame and loss that they did not make better use of their time on earth.

For the unbeliever, judgment depends entirely upon works. He has a general knowledge of God from the creation of the world and has either expressly or by implication chosen to reject God. He is therefore without any excuse.

'The wrath of God is being revealed from heaven against all the godlessness and wickedness of men who suppress the truth by their wickedness, since what may be known about God is plain to them, because God has made it plain to them. For since the creation of the world, God's invisible qualities – his eternal power and divine nature – have been clearly seen, being understood from what has been made, so that men are without any excuse.'

(Romans 1:18–20)

God will judge according to the truth (Romans 2:2), by what each person has done (Romans 2:6) and by the law if he has heard it and by the law written on his heart and his conscience if he has not heard the law (Romans 2:12–15).

The second death is when there is a final and irreversible separation of the righteous from the wicked. The wicked are cast into hell after the judgment of the Great White Throne (Revelation 21:8).

Having a knowledge of the elementary teachings about Christ will be a sure foundation for spiritual growth and should spur the believer on towards maturity.

After grasping the first principles of God's word, take solid food. Desire to discover the deeper things of God, to learn the truth and to communicate it to others. Do not be like the Corinthian Church which Paul rebuked.

> *'Brothers, I could not address you as spiritual but as worldly – mere infants in Christ. I gave you milk, not solid food, for you were not yet ready for it. Indeed, you are still not ready. You are still worldly.'*
>
> (1 Corinthians 3:1–3)

When you started to learn to swim your mother or father would have taken you to the shallow end of the swimming pool. You would have put your feet on the bottom of the pool and felt secure. Gradually, as you become used to the water and discovered how to swim you would have ventured into deeper water. When you could swim well, it is likely that you would have preferred to spend time in the deep end. Thereafter, it could be dull spending a lot of time in the shallow end.

When we are young spiritually, it is normal to learn the elementary teachings in the Bible, but after a length of time (which is different for each of us) stagnation may set in if we do not move on to something more challenging. Searching the Scriptures may be like looking for gold. There may be real struggles at times but the rewards are great and they will last forever. Daniel praised God for revealing the deep and hidden things (Daniel 2:22).

> *'The Spirit searches all things, even the deep things of God.'* (1 Corinthians 2:10)

Seeing things from God's point of view, allowing God to change the way you perceive things and finding peace and security as you meditate on the words of the Bible are all part of the hidden riches to be discovered.

How do we grow?

By serving as a member of the church in the community. We should not be content just receiving. Find out where there is a need and meet it. Find out something you like doing and do it, however small it may be. It is better to do a little well than to spread yourself too widely. There are always needs and shortages in the church.

Prefer to serve rather than be served.

> *'For even the Son of Man did not come to be served, but to serve, and to give his life as a ransom for many.'* (Mark 10:45)

Desire holiness rather than happiness. True happiness results from holiness.

What makes you happy? What makes you unhappy?

Show the fruit of the Spirit in your life and you are on the right path.

'But the fruit of the Spirit is love, joy, peace, patience, kindness, goodness, faithfulness, gentleness and self-control.' (Galatians 5:22–23)

Show commitment in everything you do. In John 15:5 Jesus describes himself as the vine and that we are the branches. To produce fruit a branch must be connected to the vine. If the branch becomes disconnected it withers and is thrown away and burned. The production of fruit is not automatic; it takes time to form. For the best fruit, vines need to be pruned (sometimes severely), fed and watered and continually looked after. Fruit goes through stages – blossom, green hard and bitter, and ripe fruit. Fruit is healthy so long as it is moving towards ripeness. A vine which does not produce good fruit will cause sadness for the vinedresser.

'Produce fruit in keeping with repentance.' (Matthew 3:8)

Chapter 8

Communication

'Then Samuel said, "Speak, for your servant is listening."' (1 Samuel 3:10)

Then the Lord told Samuel that he was going to do something in Israel which would make the ears of everyone who heard it tingle. He, the Lord, was going to punish the House of Eli for its sin, and the guilt of it would never be forgiven by sacrifice or offering. Samuel listened, but was afraid to tell Eli the vision. The following morning Eli insisted that Samuel communicate the vision. Samuel reluctantly told Eli everything, hiding nothing from him (1 Samuel 3:11–18).

Communication is the exchange of information. It can be on a one-to-one level or on a one-to-many level. It can take many forms, for example – conversation, correspondence, news, articles, books and talks.

Most people seem to enjoy listening to a good story, especially children. What makes a good story? It needs to be simple, entertaining and easy to listen to. It should have a introduction to set the scene, followed by action which builds up into a climax and a conclusion. The success of a story will depend upon a number of factors:

1. The teller – his knowledge and enthusiasm, his tone of voice and delivery, the amount and quality of preparation which he has put in, his experience, eye contact and facial expression.
2. The listener – his relationship with the teller, his age and relevant concentration span, his involvement in the story and personal contact, the culture, the environment and whether there are any distractions.

As the teller unfolds his story, he is wondering how it will be received. He wants feedback. Is the listener really listening? Are there any interruptions, yawns or fidgeting? A little humour can often regain the listener's attention. Questions afterwards will indicate how well the listener has understood the point of the story and how well it will be remembered.

Children like to be involved in the telling of a story, asking questions and having things pointed out and explained. Otherwise, their attention can easily be lost. Adults are able to sit still in silence for longer periods of time, but this does not necessarily mean that they are listening any better.

It is normally helpful for the speaker to know what effect his words has had on his listeners. He will need to ask himself the following questions:

1. Did the words achieve the goals which he was aiming for?
2. Were the words clear?
3. Were the goals realistic or were they set too high or too low?
4. For how long was it appropriate to speak?
5. For how long did the speaker retain the attention and interest of his listeners?
6. At what points (if any) did he lose the concentration of his listeners?

Where speakers ask these questions of themselves honestly and find out the answers, communication skills are likely to improve to the benefit of both the speaker and his listeners. Feedback and appraisal are healthy, provided they are done in a positive way and with sensitivity, avoiding damaging criticism.

The importance of communication is underestimated both in society and in the Church. Every day people are making assumptions, some of which are accurate, some of which are not. Where false assumptions are made problems occur for both the speaker and the listener. People need to learn how to express themselves clearly and to listen carefully.

Good communication usually leads to clarity and understanding. It builds up trust and faith and enhances good relationships.

Bad communication can lead to uncertainty and worry, misunderstandings and mistrust, deception and bad relationships.

There are many reasons for a failure to communicate (non-communication) or to communicate badly (ineffective communication) – arrogance, bad habits, bad manners, deception, dishonesty, fear, greed, guilt, ignorance, indifference, insensitivity, jealousy, lack of confidence, lack of time, laziness, pride, rudeness, unkindness and worry.

One of the main consequences of bad communication is a hindering of relationships. Bad relationships need to be put right at an early stage wherever possible so that they do not deteriorate further. We all need to be rebuked from time to time. This may provide the necessary jolt to alert us of a wrong attitude and could lead to an improvement. When this happens we should be thankful to our critic! This is what friends are for.

> *'He who listens to a life-giving rebuke*
>   *will be at home among the wise.'*   (Proverbs 15:31)

The trouble is that sin spoils and blocks communication with God and with people. Imagine that God's resources are like a deep reservoir full of fresh water. Into that reservoir are connected countless pipes, one of which leads to your heart. That pipe can be divided into sections. The section leading out of the reservoir represents freedom, the next section, healing, the next section, reconciliation, the next section, forgiveness and the final section, closest to the heart, repentance. It is God's will that pure, fresh water flows through the sections of the pipe to the heart to cleanse it and keep it clean. However, sections of the pipe become blocked up by sin which builds up. This slows down the flow of fresh water which becomes dirty, impure and contaminated.

The power of the Gospel is to deal with sin and to break down and remove the blockages in the pipe. It is important to start unblocking the pipe at the end closest to the heart, beginning with repentance and then moving on to forgiveness and reconciliation. It is unrealistic to start at the reservoir end of the pipe with freedom and healing. It is as the blockages are being removed that the water of life will start to flow more easily. This is not instantaneous. There is a lot of hard work to be done, especially where the blockages have been building up for years. It requires a change of attitude and direction to improve communication.

It is the blood of Jesus which cleanses us from sin, although our character still needs to be changed through Christ's Spirit within us.

> *'But if we walk in the light, as he is in the light, we have*
> *fellowship with one another, and the blood of Jesus, his*

Son, purifies us from all sin. If we claim to be without sin, we deceive ourselves and the truth is not in us. If we confess our sins, he is faithful and just and will forgive us our sins and purify us from all unrighteousness.'

(1 John 1:7–9)

'In fact, the law requires that nearly everything be cleansed with blood, and without the shedding of blood there is no forgiveness.'
(Hebrews 9:22)

Today a great emphasis is placed on personal hygiene. This is reflected in the vast choice of soaps, deodorants and perfumes available. Each day we need to wash our bodies to keep clean and to apply sprays, powders, oils and other substances to be fresh. If similar importance were attached to keeping the mind pure, then we would take a great deal more care, in what we say, in how we spend our time and how we treat others.

Communication exists at different levels. On a superficial level we greet each other politely and talk about the weather. At this level very little information is exchanged. Then we can talk about facts and figures which are more interesting, but not usually personal. Communication becomes harder when we express our thoughts, beliefs and feelings.

Some people find it difficult to express themselves in words, some lack confidence, others fear rejection. It may be easier to sulk, brood or become angry inside than to express feelings within us in an acceptable way. Making the effort to communicate better will often result in deeper and richer relationships.

Good communication is a skill that needs to be learned. Role models play an important part in who we are, how we think and how we behave. For the young child, mother and father are the main role models. If parents set a good example, then the child is likely to follow. Good communication skills (as well as bad communication) will be picked up and copied by the child. Where parents spend a great deal of time listening to and understanding their child, they will develop a close relationship, and create an environment where their child will be encouraged to express thoughts and feelings and gain confidence. At school, teachers set the example whilst peer groups are often bad influences. It is often said that when a child has grown up that child remembers much more what his or her teachers were like than what he or she was taught.

> *'Train a child in the way he should go,*
> *and when he is old he will not turn from it.'*
>
> (Proverbs 22:6)

> *'He who walks with the wise grows wise,*
> *but a companion of fools suffers harm.'*
>
> (Proverbs 13:20)

Communication can be difficult where there is conflict and we all face conflict from time to time. It can be difficult to forecast how people react when there is disagreement. Some people take it in their stride; for others it can lead to anger, resentment, fear and rejection.

- How do you handle conflict?
- How easy do you find it talking to people about things which they have done or said to upset you?
- Do you try and avoid arguments?
- Do you lose your temper easily?

> *'Any fool can start arguments; the honourable thing is to stay out of them.'* (Proverbs 20:3 GNB)

'The start of an argument is like the first break in a dam;
stop it before it goes any further.'

(Proverbs 17:14 GNB)

There are times when there is no alternative but to face
conflict head on.

What is your attitude when faced with this situation?

– Do you try and avoid conflict at all costs?
– Do you seek always to win the argument even when
  you are on weak ground?
– How far do you give way or stand your ground when
  you are sure that you are in the right?
– Do you look for ways of compromise to resolve
  issues?
– Are you someone who works for unity and tries to
  find common ground in a difficult situation?

Conflicts can be reduced by good communication
skills. Be prepared to actually listen to what the other
person has to say. Then try to respond properly in an
understanding way. If you cannot speak to a person face
to face, there is always the telephone or letter writing. If
someone has taken the trouble to write you a letter, do
reply to it within a reasonable period of time. It is
polite to do so and, even if you cannot, at least acknow-
ledge the letter, saying when you will respond or why
it is difficult for you to do so. Procrastination usually
makes the situation worse. Feelings of rejection and a
loss of sense of value frequently follow from poor
communication.

It is possible to resolve problems which cause upset and
hurt in a manner which enables you to sort out misunderstandings and conflict. This is done by learning to
see the point of view of the other person. As you do so
you will feel better and may be able to help others do the
same.

> *'If it is possible, as far as it depends on you, live at peace with everyone.'* (Romans 12:18)

One of the major stumbling blocks to good communication is pride. It should never be underestimated and lies in both the believer and unbeliever. It is much easier to recognise in someone else than in yourself!

> *'The pride of your heart has deceived you.'* (Obadiah v. 3)

Pride is defined in the Oxford Dictionary as:

> 'The overwhelming opinion of one's own qualities, arrogant, over-bearing attitude or conduct.'

Pride is an unattractive quality. It says, 'I am right no matter what!' It is unable to listen or to discern. It is self-reliant and contemptuous of others and of correction. Vulnerability to pride comes when things are going well.

Pride is closely linked to arrogance:

> 'The unwillingness to be questioned or criticised, opposed or checked.'

Unless there is a willingness to listen to others and accept criticism, both pride and arrogance can lead to being deceived.

The Bible has numerous examples of important and powerful people who suffered from pride. We can learn much from their attitudes and behaviour.

Naaman suffered from pride. When the prophet Elisha told him through a messenger to go and wash himself in the River Jordan, so that he would be healed of his leprosy, Naaman went away angry. He was expecting

Elisha to conduct a ceremony befitting a man of his importance. Why should he (the commander of the army of the king of Aram) wash himself in the Jordan when Abana and Pharpar (rivers in Damascus) were better? When Naaman had calmed down, he at least listened to the advice of his servants. They managed to persuade him to do what Elisha had said. Naaman became cured of his leprosy. The story is found in 2 Kings Chapter 5.

It is hard to find a more godly person in the Old Testament than King Hezekiah who did not follow the appalling example of his father King Ahaz.

> '*Hezekiah trusted in the Lord, the God of Israel. There was no-one like him among all the kings of Judah, either before him or after him. He held fast to the Lord and did not cease to follow him; he kept the commands the Lord had given Moses.*'   (2 Kings 18: 5–6)

When Jerusalem was threatened with attack from the King of Assyria, instead of making a bargain with him, King Hezekiah sought God and took counsel from the prophet Isaiah. Hezekiah trusted God and prayed that Jerusalem would not be handed over to the King of Assyria. His prayer was answered (2 Kings Chapters 18–19).

Later on, when Hezekiah was ill and on the point of death, he pleaded with God that he should not die, asking God to remember how he had served God whole-heartedly. He wept bitterly. God heard Hezekiah's prayer and spoke through Isaiah saying that fifteen years would be added to his life. Yet, surprisingly, by the end of his life Hezekiah suffered from pride.

When news of Hezekiah's illness and recovery reached Babylon, the son of the king of Babylon sent a gift. Hezekiah welcomed the royal envoys gladly and showed them his vast wealth and his arsenal of weapons (not wise to show your enemy your armoury!).

Afterwards, God rebuked Hezekiah through Isaiah. Hezekiah was told that a time would come when everything in his palace would be carried off to Babylon. Nothing would be left and even some of his own flesh and blood would be taken away.

Hezekiah's response was that the word of the Lord was good. He understood there would be peace and security in his lifetime (Isaiah 39:8). It was a very selfish response. Here was a king who had walked close with God for a large part of his life and yet at the end had fallen away. When challenged about this by Isaiah, he showed no repentance or humility in his heart. All Hezekiah could think of was his own success, importance and well-being. Some may argue that Hezekiah was just foolish, but it is hard to imagine that God would have delivered such a strong message through Isaiah if it had been foolishness alone (Isaiah chapters 38–39).

The disciples suffered from pride in the form of boasting. They had become conceited. At the end of a busy day whilst they were walking on the road to Capernaum, the disciples were arguing as to which one of them was the greatest. As the argument grew louder and became more heated, they would have raised their voices. Maybe they thought that one day, Jesus would become a very important and famous person and this would mean that they would become important and famous too.

Jesus must have made them feel uneasy and ashamed by his response:

> ' "If anyone wants to be first, he must be the very last, and the servant of all."
>
> He took a little child and had him stand among them. Taking him in his arms, he said to them,

"Whoever welcomes one of these little children in my name welcomes me; and whoever welcomes me does not welcome me but the one who sent me."'

(Mark 9:35–37)

The disciples must have been stunned. In those days children had a low status in society. They were considered unimportant and insignificant. Nowadays, attitudes are rather different and Jesus might have chosen someone who was unemployed or homeless.

Pride is an obstacle in the way of good communication. It can cause arguments and unease. Where it emerges in you, deal with it at an early stage, before it becomes a major problem.

Your motives and attitudes govern your thoughts, words and actions. They come from within.

'Therefore, as God's chosen people, holy and dearly loved, clothe yourselves with compassion, kindness, humility, gentleness and patience. Bear with each other and forgive whatever grievances you may have against one another. Forgive as the Lord forgave you. And over all these virtues put on love, which binds them all together in perfect unity.' (Colossians 3:12–14)

Conclusion

'The fruit of the righteous is a tree of life...'
(Proverbs 11:30)

Have you ever stopped to look closely at a fully mature oak tree in the middle of summer? Have you wondered how many leaves there are on its branches and how many acorns will be produced? Have you thought what is likely to happen to those acorns?

A wise man mediates and reflects. His wisdom and strength come from his relationship with God. His foundations for living are rooted in the Bible. He is no fool. He learns from his mistakes. He grows when things are going well and also through difficulties. He perseveres.

> *'Blessed is the man*
> *who does not walk in the counsel of the wicked*
> *or stand in the way of sinners*
> *or sit in the seat of mockers.*
> *But his delight is in the law of the LORD,*
> *and on his law he meditates day and night.*
> *He is like a tree planted by streams of water,*
> *which yields its fruit in season*
> *and whose leaf does not wither.*
> *Whatever he does prospers.'*   (Psalm 1:1–3)

The front cover of this book pictures the potential of the acorn to develop into an oak tree. The eight chapters are to encourage you to have a new beginning, to grow towards maturity and to be fruitful in your life.

As you look around the countryside, you will see all the different stages of growth. The most important thing is to be growing. When you next look at an oak tree, think back to its beginning.